MEDITATE

★ A GUIDED JOURNAL ★

Original book design by Debbie Berne Design
Cover and journal design by Laura H. Couallier, Laura Herrmann Design
Photography and illustrations from istockphoto.com, Thinkstock.com,
Fotolia.com, and Shutterstock.com

Printed and bound in China

MEDITATE
☆ A GUIDED JOURNAL ☆

DR. MARTIN HART & SKYE ALEXANDER

FAIR WINDS
PRESS
BEVERLY, MASSACHUSETTS

HOW TO USE THIS JOURNAL

When you meditate, you stop thinking about work, relationships, finances, and daily chores, and become present in the moment. Mental chatter ceases temporarily and you experience a state of relaxation in both mind and body.

During meditation, the brain also steps up production of endorphins, the proteins that enhance positive feelings. According to a recent clinical trial of 97,000 subjects conducted by the Women's Health Initiative, positive, optimistic people enjoy longer, healthier lives than their negative, pessimistic peers.

This journal can serve as a record of what transpired during your meditations. Include everything you experienced sensually—sights, sounds, tactile experiences, tastes, scents. Write the "story" of what happened. Most important, write what you felt. Feel it as you write it. Did anger come up? Anxiety? Serenity? Joy? Write it all down. You could even include a drawing of the meditation. All this helps bring unconscious information to your conscious mind, and eventually into your conscious experience. Above all, enjoy—no strain, no struggle, no stress; just fun.

Prepare to Meditate

Meditating is easy. It does not involve complicated rituals or specially designed environments. You don't need any tools or accoutrements. You don't have to sit in funny positions or burn incense (unless you want to). All you need is a comfortable place to sit or lie down. You can meditate any time of the day or night, at home or work, indoors or outside, alone or with other people. Give yourself a little bit of quiet, private time. Twenty-five to forty minutes a day is ideal, but if in the beginning you can only devote ten minutes to meditation, that's fine. You'll still see results. The following suggestions will help make the experience go more smoothly for you.

Close your eyes and use your imagination to create an inner place of peace and security that's private and tranquil, a place no one can enter unless invited in by you. You can remember a special place from your past, choose a place in your current life, recall one from a photo or movie you've seen—or make it up entirely. What does it look like? Notice the details of your surroundings. Is it by an ocean or high up in the mountains? Are there trees and flowers? Do your senses pick up anything else? Does your Safe Place have a pleasant fragrance? What does the air feel like on your skin? There is no right or wrong. This is a Safe Place created by you, for you. You'll go to this place each time you meditate, and return from it once your inner journey has ended. This Safe Place is one you create—no one should create it for you.

☆ The Safe Place must be in nature. Do not imagine forts, buildings, castles, public structures, and so on; these suggest to your unconscious that you are in "defense mode," not a spot where you feel safe, relaxed, and at peace.

☆ Use the same Safe Place to begin every directed inward meditation. Changing from place to place tells the unconscious you are unsure, scattered, insecure, or inconsistent.

☆ Each time you meditate, notice a little more about this wondrous place you've chosen. Observe its beauty. Remember the saying, "Love pays attention to detail." Maybe you see a plant or shrub you never paid attention to before. What about that rock? Use your inner senses. What fragrances do you smell? What does this place taste like? Reach out and touch things. Listen to the sounds around you.

Before doing any of the directed inward meditations in this book, we recommend that you spend some time—perhaps fifteen to twenty minutes each day for a week—in this Safe Place within yourself. You needn't "see" this place clearly.

Perceiving it with any of your senses will suffice. The most important thing is to feel its safety and security. Know that you belong here.

Handling Resistances

The three most common obstacles to meditation are the following:

☆ Falling asleep during meditation
☆ Too many thoughts
☆ Procrastination

All these are resistances, and all come from one source: fear. Here's an example of how resistance works. Let's say you want to leave an unhappy relationship. But you're afraid of being alone, or fear you won't be able to support yourself financially, or believe the end of a relationship means you're a failure. Your resistance kicks in. You procrastinate. You distract yourself with work or other activities. You tune out (figuratively fall asleep). Meditation lets you become aware of your feelings and motivations—and your resistance—so you can take responsibility for acting on that awareness.

Instead of trying to "overcome" resistances to fear, which would perpetuate the distorted ideas linking power with aggression, we would be better served by acknowledging our fear, recognizing where it is coming from, attending to it, and releasing it. The following suggestions can help you work with resistance:

FALLING ASLEEP

☆ Before meditating, close your eyes and, as best you can, become still. In whatever state of calmness you feel, mentally reassure your frightened "younger selves" (the inner children in which the fear resides) that everything will be fine; you (the adult) are here, won't leave, and will keep them safe.

☆ Sit instead of lying down to meditate. If that doesn't work, try standing against a wall while holding on to a chair. It might seem strange at first, but it's hard to fall asleep in a standing position.

TOO MANY THOUGHTS

☆ Close your eyes and, as best you can, become still. In whatever state of calmness you feel, mentally reassure your frightened "younger selves" that everything will be fine; you (the adult) are here, won't leave, and will keep them safe.

☆ Pay attention to the resistance you experience. Be honest with yourself. Write your feelings down in your meditation journal.

☆ Do not force yourself to sit and meditate. Instead, try doing one of the active "waking" meditations, such as taking a walk in nature.

☆ Ask your Higher Self to heal the resistance and lift it from you while you meditate. (This should not be a substitute for processing through your fear after the meditation is over.)

PROCRASTINATION

☆ If you're too busy to meditate, you're too busy.

☆ Discipline yourself. Establish a time to meditate and stick to it. Make meditation part of your daily routine.

☆ Remove distractions. Turn off the TV. Spend less time at the computer.

☆ Ask your Higher Self to heal the resistances. Everything is a product of your intention and what you give attention to. If you truly want to meditate and devote your attention to it, the resistance will be but a brief nuisance. Ask your Higher Self for help—the answer will always be "yes."

"Go into yourself and see how deep the place is from which your life flows."

~ *Rainer Maria Rilke*

MEDITATIONS FOR
RELAXATION AND
STRESS RELIEF

Practice Polarity Breathing to Sleep Better

Based on an ancient yogic breathing technique, this will balance the body's yin (receptive/passive) and yang (assertive/active) energies and produce a calm, tranquil state. Practice this technique every night when you go to bed to help you relax and sleep better.

———∘O∘———

Lie on your back, with eyes closed. With your right thumb, gently close off your right nostril. Breathe slowly and deeply through your left nostril. Inhale, letting breath fill your abdomen first, then your chest. Exhale, expelling air from your chest first, then your abdomen, until all breath is released. ✴ Repeat for about a minute. Pay attention to your breathing. ✴ Repeat with left thumb over left nostril for about a minute. ✴ If your mind starts to wander, gently bring it back to your breathing. Feel your breath circulating through your body. Feel your mind and body gradually relaxing, as your system comes into harmony. ✴ Switch nostrils again. Do this for as long as is comfortable, or until you fall asleep.

Few Westerners knew much about meditation until 1959, when the Indian teacher Maharishi Mahesh Yogi introduced Transcendental Meditation (TM) to the United States. Based in the Vedic tradition, TM uses a mantra to induce relaxation and transcend thinking.

WHAT ARE CHAKRAS?

Healing and balancing the chakras is an objective of many holistic healing therapies. *Chakra* is a Sanskrit term meaning wheel. To sensitive individuals who can see them, these nonphysical energy centers resemble spinning wheels located roughly along the spine. The life force travels up the spinal column and energizes these vortices.

Each chakra is associated with certain parts of the body. When the chakras become blocked or don't operate properly, illness occurs. Health and happiness result when the life force flows freely and harmoniously through the chakras.

Crown chakra

Brow chakra

Throat chakra

Heart chakra

Solar plexus chakra

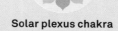

Sacral chakra

Root chakra

Many healing traditions, such as Ayurvedic medicine and homeopathy, assert that all discomfort and disease have their source in the unconscious, and eventually emerge into consciousness or our four-square reality as some form of mental, emotional, or physical ailment or imbalance.

Relieve Computer-Related Tension

Sitting at a computer for hours on end puts pressure on your neck and shoulders. This "waking" meditation, or directed, outward form of meditation, loosens tight muscles, relaxes your mind, and relieves general tension.

———∘O∘———

Sit in a comfortable position and close your eyes. Keep your back straight, your shoulders down. Inhale slowly and deeply as you gently turn your head to the left, stretching your neck just to the point where you feel your muscles begin to resist. ✶ Exhale slowly as you gently turn your head to the right, stretching your neck just to the point where you feel your muscles begin to resist. Repeat. This time, stretch your neck a little further, but don't go beyond your point of comfort. ✶ Move slowly and deliberately—don't hurry or jerk—stretching your muscles only as far as feels comfortable. ✶ Inhale slowly and deeply, filling your stomach with air first, then your chest. ✶ Exhale slowly, releasing air from your chest first, then your stomach. ✶ Continue gently turning your head from one side to the other, inhaling as you turn to the left and exhaling as you turn to the right. Keep your mind calm and still. ✶ Continue doing this for as long as you like. When you feel looser and more relaxed, open your eyes.

THE DIFFERENT CHAKRAS

Root chakra—located at the base of the spine, this energy center is associated with the survival instinct and your sense of security.

Sacral chakra—found near the abdomen in the vicinity of the lower back, about a hand's width below the belly button, this chakra is related to creativity and sexuality.

Solar plexus chakra—located at the solar plexus, about halfway between your belly button and heart, this chakra is connected with the will and personal power.

....

....

....

....

....

....

....

....

....

....

....

....

....

Heart chakra—situated near the heart, this chakra regulates the heart, blood circulation, skin, chest, and upper back.

Throat chakra—found at the base of the neck, between the collarbones, this chakra is associated with self-expression and communication.

Brow chakra—located on the forehead between the eyebrows, at the site of the "third eye," this chakra is the center of intuition.

Crown chakra—situated at the top of the head, the crown chakra is associated with the soul and your connection to the Divine.

Turn Down the Annoyance Level
in Your Environment

This meditation technique helps you deal with annoying people, workplace
noise, and other stress by turning down the volume.

———o0o———

Isolate a particular noise that you find annoying. Focus on that noise for
a moment, trying to distinguish it from other sounds in your environment.
* Close your eyes and take a few slow, deep breaths. Bring to mind an image
of a large, round dial. This dial controls the volume of the noise that you find
annoying. Make the dial a bright color, such as red or orange. * Imagine
yourself reaching to grasp that dial. Take hold of the dial and begin slowly
turning it to lower the volume. As you adjust the dial, notice the color starts to
fade and become softer. See the dial change color. Watch it shift to a peaceful
pale blue. As you turn the dial, you ratchet down the volume of the annoying
noise. * Continue turning the dial, lowering the noise level a little at a time. Feel
yourself growing calmer and more relaxed. Sense yourself detaching
from the annoying noise, until the sound no longer seems as bothersome.
* Keep turning down the volume until the noise becomes tolerable
or even diminishes entirely from your awareness.

According to the American Institute of Stress, workplace stress costs the United States $300 billion annually in medical care and employee absenteeism. A three-month study, published in 1993 in the journal Anxiety, Stress, & Coping, examined workers in the automotive industry to determine the effects of meditation on stress reduction. The study found that employees who meditated regularly experienced decreases in job tension, anxiety, fatigue, and health complaints.

Meditation Accomplishes Three Things

* It attracts things into your life.
* It removes things from your life.
* It makes you aware of your resistance to allowing the first two to happen.

Health insurance statistics showed that people who meditated regularly had significantly fewer inpatient and outpatient hospital visits than non-meditators.

MEDITATIONS FOR
PHYSICAL HEALING

Breathe Deeply to Lower Your Blood Pressure

The American Heart Association's journal Hypertension reported in November 1995 and August 1996 that meditation can be as effective as antihypertensive drugs in reducing blood pressure in both men and women—without the unwanted side effects.

————o0o————

Lie on your back in a quiet place where you feel safe and comfortable. Put a pillow under your knees to elevate them slightly. Place your right palm on your abdomen, and lay your left arm along your side, palm facing up. ✷ Close your eyes and begin breathing slowly and deeply. Turn your attention to your breathing. As you inhale, count slowly to six. Fill your stomach with air first. Feel your stomach rise as it expands to take in oxygen-rich air. Continue inhaling slowly, filling your lungs with air. ✷ When you feel full, hold your breath for a count of four. Exhale slowly, to a count of six. Release the air from your lungs and chest first, then your stomach. Pull your stomach in toward your backbone, emptying yourself completely of air. Repeat, keeping your attention focused on your breathing. ✷ If distracting thoughts come into your mind, simply let them go without judgment, and return your attention to your breathing. Feel yourself simultaneously becoming more relaxed, centered, and revitalized. ✷ Continue breathing in this manner for at least ten minutes.

Meditation only takes a short period of time each day, costs absolutely nothing, requires no special equipment or accoutrements, and can be done successfully by anyone, anywhere, anytime. Meditation could be the single most valuable tool we have available to heal ourselves and our planet.

WHAT'S YOUR FAVORITE ELEMENT?

Air, fire, water, or earth?

When you are in the presence of this element do you feel more at peace, more connected to your Soul and Spirit? Perhaps you feel more alive near a lake, a river, or the ocean. Or maybe walking in the woods is an enchanting experience for you. Do you feel a sense of liberation when standing high on a hill with the wind at your face? Or a special connection with a burning fire?

During meditation, your heart rate and respiration slow. Brain wave frequencies slow from the usual 13 to 30 cycles per second (the beta, or active, outwardly focused, level of consciousness) to 8 to 13 cps (the alpha level, a more inwardly focused, expanded state of awareness). Brain wave activity also shifts from the right frontal cortex to the left.

Apply Loving Hands to Ease Pain

The purpose of pain is to warn you that something needs attention—yes, something physical, but in a more real sense, something emotional. The following meditation can ease discomfort while you're healing.

———o○o———

Sit or lie comfortably, with your eyes closed. Take a deep breath and exhale. Do this two more times. After you are somewhat relaxed, mentally count down from seven to one, relaxing more deeply with each count. ✷ On the count of one, find yourself in your Safe Place at evening time. Use your inner sense(s) to make this place more real to you. ✷ Notice your Higher Self standing by a "healing bed." It might be a soft bed of flowers, silk or satin, or perhaps downy feathers. Sense this healing place as comfortable, beautiful, enchanting, magical, and loving. ✷ Approach your Higher Self. Stand facing each other. Feel your Higher Self's love for you. Let your Higher Self lovingly and gently remove your clothes and lower you onto the bed. ✷ Close your mental eyes and feel the stillness. Higher Self gently places its hand(s) upon your pain, sending a soothing warm light to you. See or sense the light surrounding the area of pain, absorbing or transmuting it. ✷ When the pain diminishes or is gone, close your mental eyes and mentally count from one to five. ✷ Open your physical eyes on the count of five.

GET TO KNOW YOUR HIGHER SELF

Within each of us is a part that transcends our conscious awareness; in this book we call that part your Higher Self. It is impossible to accurately describe the Higher Self in words or to comprehend it fully. You could think of it as the part of you that is always in communication with Spirit, God, Goddess, Buddha, or something else. The Higher Self is the highest expression of you, or as physics would describe it, a higher resonance of you.

Heal Hidden Issues with Chakra Light

Your unconscious knows the origins of all health problems, as well as what's needed for their resolution. Allow your unconscious to determine which chakra influence is needed to heal your condition. In this meditation, don't try to determine what's supposed to happen—just let it come.

———∘O∘———

Sit or lie comfortably, with your eyes closed. Take a deep breath and exhale. Do this two more times. After you are somewhat relaxed, mentally count down from seven to one, relaxing more deeply with each count. ✻ On the count of one, find yourself in your Safe Place. Invite your Higher Self to join you in this place. Sit together. Be together. Love together. ✻ When you've finished, lie down in your Safe Place and close your mental eyes. Let your attention go to the site of your physical ailment. A sphere of light will appear. It will be the color of one of the seven chakras: red, orange, yellow, green, blue, indigo, or white. Do not judge or manipulate it. ✻ The sphere of light will surround and bathe the ailing part of your body in its healing light, flowing around and through this area. Feel it! In time, the sphere will be absorbed in and around the body part or region. Open your mental eyes. ✻ Let your Higher Self hold you, love you, and heal you. Thank your Higher Self and close your mental eyes again. Count mentally from one to five. On the count of five, open your physical eyes and return.

Sometimes, hidden issues cause imbalances that overlap and express in parts of the body that may seem unrelated. Let's say, for example, that you have a diagnosed heart condition. The heart is influenced by the fourth, or "heart," chakra. But, if you feel insecure and fearful about love, this "overlap energy" could be sending you a signal. The healing solution could be to shine the light of the first chakra (the security center) onto your heart.

Conscious, Subconscious, and Unconscious Minds

The conscious mind calibrates and constructs all that you sense outside of yourself.

The subconscious mind holds the myriad beliefs, templates, and instructions you've accumulated as a result of your lifetime experiences. It filters opportunities that present themselves, and either allows them in or rejects them. For example, if at the age of fifteen you placed into your subconscious the instruction "I'll never love like that again," when the opportunity for love presents itself at age forty-two, the subconscious instruction (unless consciously removed) will kick in and sabotage the opportunity.

The unconscious mind transcends the conscious and subconscious, yet it includes these parts as well. Everything is contained in the unconscious. If you liken the conscious mind to planet Earth, the subconscious would be our solar system, and the unconscious would be all possible universes.

Meditation invites unconscious issues to surface
so you can address them consciously.
This is the principal healing benefit of meditation.

MEDITATIONS FOR
EMOTIONAL
HEALING

Burn Incense to Calm Anxiety

Incense burning began in Japan around 600 C.E. Because inhaling aromatic substances affects the limbic system of the brain, the seat of emotions, burning the types of incense listed in this meditation can also help ease anxiety.

———o○o———

Choose incense made of pure plant materials and free of artificial ingredients. Choose incense in one or more of the following scents: sandalwood, lavender, vanilla, frankincense, clary sage, bergamot, or benzoin. ✿ Fit the incense in a fireproof burner, and light it. Blow out the flame and let the incense slowly smolder, emitting fragrant smoke into the air. Set the incense where it can burn safely. ✿ Sit or lie in a place where you feel safe and comfortable, several feet away from the incense. Close your eyes and relax using whichever method you prefer. Focus your attention on the aroma. ✿ As you inhale, feel the soothing scent calming your brain, silencing all thoughts and worries. As you exhale, feel the tension in your chest and abdomen relax as the anxiety leaves your body. ✿ Continue breathing in this manner for at least ten minutes, or as long as is comfortable for you, keeping your attention focused on inhaling and exhaling the pleasing aroma. When you feel ready, open your eyes.

Meditation's popularity grew throughout the 1960s, due in part to the influence of the Beatles, who had studied with Maharishi in India. During the next fifty years, Maharishi trained forty thousand teachers, who took the TM technique to more than five million people worldwide.

ANGER MANAGEMENT

As stress increases in our lives, so do anger and aggression. More than 25,000 murders are committed in the United States annually. In the workplace, five million people are assaulted each year, according to the Bureau of Labor Statistics. Add to those figures domestic violence, road rage, and other violent expressions of anger and it's apparent we need a strategy for anger management. The meditation below helps defuse anger by enabling you to detach from exterior stimuli.

Destructive emotions are any emotions—positive or negative—that you don't allow yourself to feel. Constructive emotions are any emotions—positive or negative—that you do allow yourself to feel, and in the case of the negative emotions, to release. Fully accessing all emotions is vital to emotional healing.

Release Unwanted Habits and Behaviors

Self-limiting behaviors such as overeating, alcoholism, obsessive-compulsive behavior, smoking, drug use, television addiction, and so on are often linked with both stress and poor self-esteem. The following meditation helps you reprogram your thinking and release unwanted attitudes and behaviors.

———o0o———

Sit or lie comfortably, with your eyes closed. After you are somewhat relaxed, mentally count down from seven to one, relaxing more deeply with each number.
✶ On the count of one, sense that you are in your Safe Place. Bring your attention to the point between your eyebrows—called the "third eye." Also known as the Asna, or brow chakra, this energy center is associated with your perceptions.
✶ Call to mind the habit, attitude, or self-limiting behavior you wish to release. Keep focusing on your brow chakra. Imagine an indigo light glowing between your eyebrows. Indigo is a color of serenity, transcendence, and transformation.
✶ Now call to mind the condition you wish to bring into your life. Feel the indigo light dissolve your resistance to releasing your old habit or behavior. Perceive yourself liberated from the self-imposed limits of this habit or behavior. Feel what you would feel having become free of it. ✶ Hold in your mind the image of the outcome you seek for as long as you can. Feel the joy, satisfaction, contentment, or whatever else you would feel when you are living the out-come. When you feel ready, mentally count from one to five. On the count of five, open your physical eyes.

ANXIETY,
STRESS, AND
COPING

A three-month study of the effects of stress, published in the journal Anxiety, Stress, & Coping in 1993, found that along with reducing stress, meditation also helped alleviate other health and lifestyle problems. Subjects who meditated regularly decreased their use of cigarettes and hard liquor (beer and wine were not mentioned in the survey) and experienced less anxiety and fatigue. As a result, their general health improved and so did their personal and work relationships.

....

....

....

....

....

....

....

....

Quiet the Voice of Fear

Fear, like pain, is a messenger. Pain tells us something physical needs attention; fear tells us something emotional needs attention. Use this meditation to face your fear, forgive it, and let it go.

———o○o———

Sit or lie comfortably, with your eyes closed. Take a deep breath and exhale. Do this two more times. After you are somewhat relaxed, mentally count down from seven to one, relaxing more deeply with each count. ✷ On the count of one, find yourself in your Safe Place. Use your inner sense(s) to make this place more real to you. Sense the beauty, love, blessed solitude, or enchantment of this place. ✷ Invite your fear to present itself to you. Allow the fear to speak. Remember, its fear is your fear. It may tell you why it's fearful. It may weep, wail, cry out in anger, or react in some other way. ✷ When it's done, when it can't speak anymore, hold it, love it, reassure it. Lovingly tell it, "You'll be fine. I will not abandon you." Remember, love is stronger than fear. Sense it becoming more relaxed and at peace. Soon, it fades away. ✷ Now, close your mental eyes and mentally count from one to five. On the count of five, open your physical eyes. Your fear will be gone or greatly lessened.

More than twenty million Americans—one in eleven—now meditate regularly.

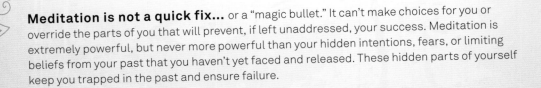

Meditation is not a quick fix... or a "magic bullet." It can't make choices for you or override the parts of you that will prevent, if left unaddressed, your success. Meditation is extremely powerful, but never more powerful than your hidden intentions, fears, or limiting beliefs from your past that you haven't yet faced and released. These hidden parts of yourself keep you trapped in the past and ensure failure.

By reducing stress, meditation can not only improve your quality of life but also can extend your life.

MEDITATIONS FOR
OVERALL HEALTH, REJUVENATION, AND LONGEVITY

Connect With the Source of All Life

This meditation affirms your spiritual existence, your eternal nature that continues even when the physical body dies, and your connection to all that is.

—○O○—

Sit, stand, or lie in a place where you feel safe and comfortable. Close your eyes, and relax using whichever method you prefer. ✶ Breathe slowly and deeply, growing more calm and serene with each breath. Focus on your breathing as you allow mundane thoughts to slip away. ✶ As you exhale, say the words "I Am." Feel your head, throat, and chest resonate with the sounds "I Am." Become aware of your link with the divine realm. ✶ Sense life energy flowing in through your crown chakra (at the top of your head) and down into your body. Inhale again and sense the breath of life connecting you with all beings on Earth. Exhale again as you intone the words "I Am." ✶ Feel the sound expand beyond your head, throat, and chest until it resonates through your entire body. Witness yourself as the spiritual being you are. ✶ When you feel ready, open your eyes. Breathe as you normally do, but retain your awareness of your spiritual nature and your connection with all that is.

During the past four decades, more than six hundred studies conducted at 250 Universities and medical schools worldwide have verified meditation's efficacy.

YOU ARE
NOT ALONE

You have never been
alone. You will never
be alone. You are part
of a multidimensional
matrix that links all of
us—humans, animals,
plants, deities, and other
nonphysical entities—to
one another, and to the
rest of the universe.

An increasing number of businesses offer meditation classes for their employees, including companies such as Apple Computer, Yahoo, Google, Raytheon, McKinsey & Company, Deutsche Bank, AOL Time Warner, and Hughes Aircraft.

Rejuvenate Your Skin

This quick and easy meditation allows you to collect healing energy in your hands and direct it to your face—or any other part of your body that requires rejuvenation.

——○O○——

Sit, stand, or lie in a place where you feel safe and comfortable. Close your eyes, and relax. Press your palms together and rub them vigorously for a few moments, until you feel them growing warm. ✷ Stop and hold them open, toward your chin, about 1 inch (5 cm) away from your face. Slowly move your hands upward from your chin to the top of your head. Feel the rejuvenating energy radiating onto your face. Imagine wrinkles, acne, or other blemishes disappearing as you direct healing energy into your skin. ✷ When you get to the top of your head, flick your hands as if you were throwing off water. Again, rub your palms together for a few moments until they feel warm. ✷ Holding your palms about 1 inch (5 cm) away from your face, again move your hands up slowly from your chin to the top of your head. When you get to the top of your head, flick your hands again. ✷ Repeat for a total of six times, or until you feel you've accomplished your objective. When you are ready, open your eyes.

Some of our inner senses are not as developed as others. Maybe you find it hard to visualize, yet you can hear, smell, touch, or even taste the inner experience. That's fine. Not being able to visualize in meditation does not limit or detract from the experience or its benefits. The most important experience you have when meditating is the experience of whatever it is you feel.

....

....

....

....

....

....

....

....

Erase Negative Thinking to Enhance Health and Longevity

Maybe Bobby McFerrin was on to something when he sang, "Don't Worry, Be Happy." The following ongoing meditation helps you become aware of your negative thoughts so you can transform them into positive ones.

——o○o——

You have the power to control your emotions with your thoughts, and you can shift unpleasant feelings to happier ones by making a conscious decision to adjust your thinking. ✶ Each time you notice yourself feeling anxious, angry, fearful, sad, discouraged, or otherwise unhappy—in the absence of any immediate, strong, and reasonable impetus—stop what you're doing and turn your attention to the feeling. ✶ Retrace your thoughts until you can connect your emotional reaction(s) to a particular thought(s). Close your eyes and bring to mind the thought that triggered your unpleasant emotional reaction. Imagine the negative thought written on a blackboard. ✶ Sense yourself picking up an eraser and erasing the thought from the blackboard. Acknowledge your power over the thought and your ability to wipe it out, so it no longer impacts your happiness and well-being. Notice how erasing this idea makes you feel. ✶ Now, shift your focus to something more positive—a memory of a pleasant experience. Notice how bringing to mind a positive memory or image shifts your emotions into a lighter, happier place. ✶ Enjoy this positive feeling for as long as you choose. When you're ready, take a deep breath and open your eyes. Each time a negative thought arises into your awareness, repeat this process.

During meditation, old templates you may have about "power" will surface to block the meditation, in the form of resistance. As humans, we all deal with fear in one or a combination of four ways: denial, discounting, defense, and distraction.

Most people who claim they cannot internally visualize actually can visualize very well. The static caused by their resistance to meditation—and more particularly, to the potential benefits they may derive from meditation—accounts for their lack of "inner seeing." Face your resistances as a separate issue; if you process through them using the methods described in this book, you'll be surprised at how well you can visualize.

In our fast-paced society, we often multitask.
When we try to do more than one thing at a time,
we only partly pay attention to what we're doing.

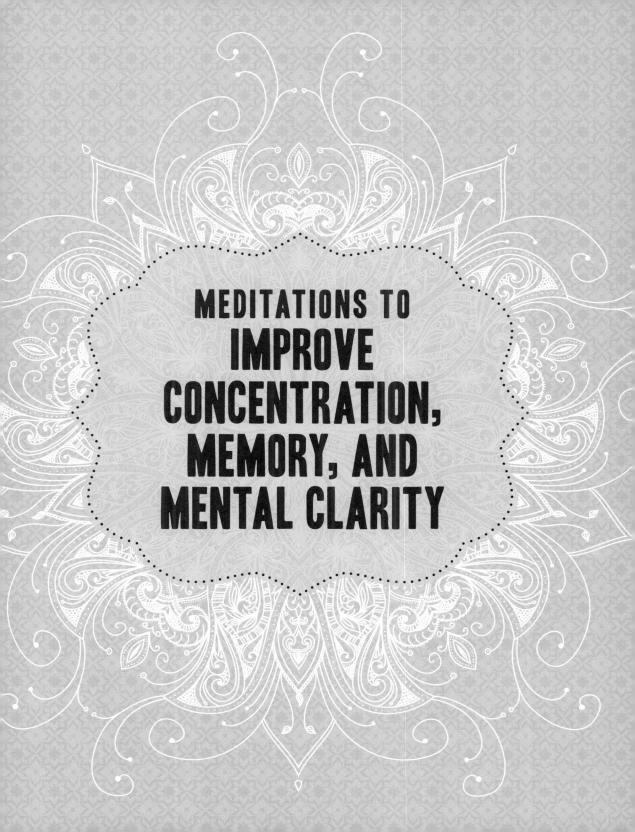

MEDITATIONS TO IMPROVE CONCENTRATION, MEMORY, AND MENTAL CLARITY

Increase Mental Clarity and Attention

The following meditation incorporates acupressure to enhance benefits. Use it to promote mental clarity, deepen concentration, and improve your ability to pay attention.

—∘O∘—

Sit in a comfortable place, with your eyes closed. Take a deep breath and exhale. Do this two more times. Relax using whichever method you prefer. * Continue breathing slowly, deeply, and rhythmically. Keep your attention focused on your breathing. * Whenever a thought arises into your awareness or your mind starts to wander, gently press your index finger to the small depression between your upper lip and the tip of your nose. Hold this acupressure point for a few moments as you release the thought from your mind.. * Return your attention to your breathing. Each time a thought intrudes into your awareness, press this point and hold it until the thought slips away. * Notice your mind growing more and more relaxed. Gradually, your meditation will deepen and thoughts will become less frequent. * Continue in this manner for as long as you like. When you feel ready, open your eyes.

Your Higher Self's awareness is greater than that of your conscious self. Working with your Higher Self will enable you to bring more awareness into your daily life.

BE SPECIFIC ABOUT WHAT YOU WANT

When meditating, instead of saying "I want to feel better," try "I want to end this headache." Instead of "I want my business to improve," think "I want twelve more sales this week." Stay within your range of belief. Don't program your mind beyond what you feel is possible. Your unconscious cannot be fooled—it will know you're just "playing around."

Mandalas are elaborate, circular images that symbolize the world. The word mandala means "circle" in Sanskrit. In some mandalas, the top hemisphere represents the heavens, the lower hemisphere the earth, signifying the interconnection between the two levels of existence.

Create a Mandala to Promote Mental Balance

Although mandalas are often painted, they can be fashioned of any material. Many contain archetypal, spiritual, or magical motifs, as well as personal ones. Your mandala should contain whatever symbols, colors, and images appeal to or have meaning for you.

———○O○———

Collect materials you'll need: paper and paste, paints and brushes, crayons or colored markers, magazine pictures, fabric, and so on. ✻ Draw a circle, as large as you like. Within the circle, sketch, paint, paste, sew, or otherwise combine images that you find appealing. You may wish to keep the image of the world or the universe in mind. The upper portion of the circle might represent the sky, the lower part the earth. Or, the upper half could symbolize the conscious mind and the outer world, the lower half the inner, subconscious dimension. ✻ As you fashion your mandala, imbue it with intention—it becomes an embodiment of your vision, feelings, and objectives. ✻ You can use the mandala as a tool for meditation. Instead of forming images in your mind, as you would during creative visualization practices, relax and gaze at the mandala. Without analysis or judgment, observe the individual images and the mandala as a whole. Notice details. Try to see beyond the obvious. See the whole as more than the sum of its parts. Pay attention to any insights or impressions that arise into your awareness. Reflect on your mandala whenever you like, for as long as you like.

Meditate at the Time That's Best for You

Meditation in the morning can affect the entire day in wonderful ways. Meditating when you get home from work or school is a good idea, too, and lets you release the stress of the day. Meditating before going to bed can be great, as long as you don't fall asleep. (If you do, try sitting up to meditate.) Meditating before bed programs the unconscious mind to work with your intention during the night.

....

....

....

....

....

....

....

....

Reduce the Symptoms of ADHD

The following active meditation is quick, easy, and effective—and kids
enjoy doing it. It also helps adults improve their concentration,
focus, and memory.

—∘O∘—

Stand with your feet together, arms at your sides. Take a few slow, deep
breaths to begin calming and centering yourself. Bring your hands up to
your chest and press your palms together as if you were praying, with
your thumbs resting against your breastbone. Choose a focal point and
train your eyes on it. ✻ Inhale as you bend your knees and squat down,
until you are in a position similar to sitting in a straight-backed chair.
Keep your back straight. Your thighs should be at a 90-degree angle to
your calves and your back. Stay in this position for a few moments.
✻ Exhale as you slowly come up to a standing position again. Repeat.
Keep your eyes on the focal point you've chosen. Pay attention to your
movements and your breath as you continue squatting and standing,
in a slow, rhythmic manner. ✻ If your mind starts to wander or thoughts
arise into your consciousness, simply let them go and return your
attention to your breath and movements.

Meditation, in its role as a doorway between the conscious, subconscious, and unconscious, allows you access to unconscious information, as dreams do.

MEDITATING WITH OTHER PEOPLE?

Meditating with other people can be a powerful experience. When you combine your meditation with that of other people who are in the same "space" as you are, the results become exponentially greater. Remember to be respectful to the others in the room and insist that they be respectful of you.

This is not a time for talking, giggling, or making any other type of noise.

Concentration is key to performance excellence
—whether you're on the playing field or in the boardroom
—and meditation is one of the best ways to
improve your concentration.

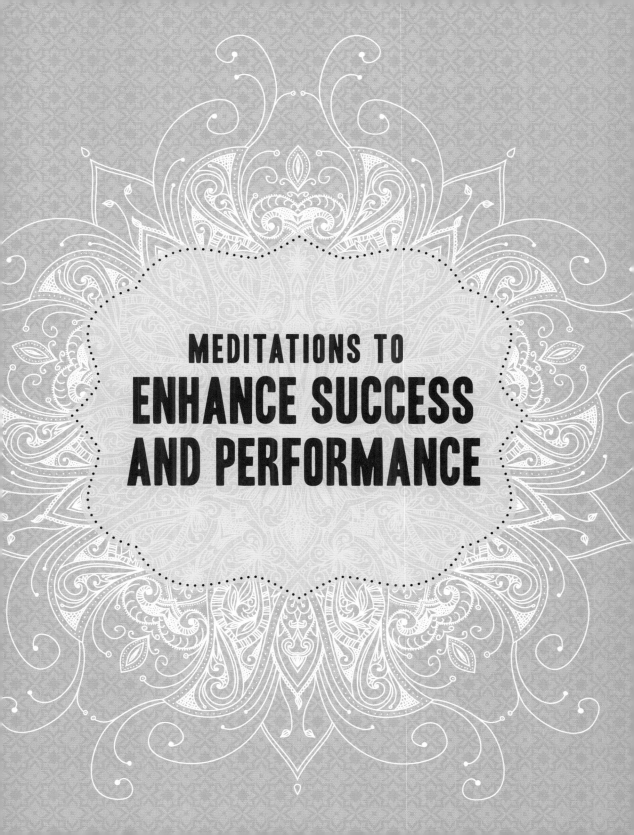

MEDITATIONS TO
ENHANCE SUCCESS
AND PERFORMANCE

Improve Your Athletic Ability

Many world-class athletes meditate, including Kobe Bryant, Michael Jordan, and Tiger Woods. Phil Jackson, head coach of the Los Angeles Lakers, meditates regularly and has encouraged members of his team to follow suit. The following meditation helps you improve your game by training your mind.

———o○o———

Sit quietly in a comfortable place and close your eyes. Take a deep breath and exhale. Repeat two more times. Imagine yourself getting ready to play your favorite sport. Feel yourself go through all the motions you normally engage in when you play your sport—but do it very slowly, paying careful attention to each movement. ✿ Bring all your senses into the experience. Make the scenario as vivid as possible. Feel your body and mind working together in complete harmony. Notice how calm, centered, and confident you are.
✿ Experience the joy of playing your sport—have fun.
Play the game in your mind for as long as you like.
When you feel ready, open your eyes.

The brain wave changes induced by meditation boost stem cell production, enhancing the body's ability to regenerate and repair itself.

TAKE TIME
AFTER YOU
MEDITATE

Allow some time after
meditation before resuming
activity. If possible, lie down
for a bit after meditating.
The transition from a state of
meditation to one of activity
should always be slow and
comfortable, even if you feel
the meditation was not that
"deep." Don't rush.

Elevating your athletic performance, as in all areas of life, requires getting out of your own way. You've probably heard the term "in the zone." Physicists call it "frictionless flow," a state in which you encounter no resistance to anything you do.

Release Performance Anxiety

Whether you have stage fright, interview anxiety, first date jitters, or any other type of performance anxiety, the following meditation will help you feel grounded, protected, and confident.

—∘O∘—

Sit quietly in a place where you feel comfortable and close your eyes. Imagine a shaft of light, like a laser beam, descending from above you. Sense it enter the crown of your head and travel down through the center of your body. ✿ Feel the light move through each chakra and then exit your tailbone region (this experience may give you quite a rush). Imagine the shaft of light continuing its descent, all the way down to the very center of the Earth. See or sense the beam grounding you as it anchors you to the Earth. ✿ Now, imagine a sphere of luminescent light forming around you, like a cocoon. This sphere shields you and provides a sense of security. From your place within the sphere, ask your Higher Self to remove the anxiety you are experiencing. ✿ Feel the sphere drawing the anxiety and tension out of you and away from you. Remain in the meditation for as long as you like. When you feel ready, open your eyes.

MEDITATE DAILY

Above all, choose to meditate every day and stick with it. Meditation's benefits are cumulative. The rewards you reap will increase with dedication and consistency. We recommend meditating once or twice per day, and not more than twice. Too much meditating can be a sign of desperation and, as such, will produce few results. Meditation works; desperation doesn't.

....

....

....

....

....

....

....

....

Improve Focus, Persistence, and Follow-Through

The following meditation uses a Zen technique of emphasizing the process instead of the goal. By keeping your attention on the task at hand, the meditation strengthens your focus, patience, and persistence.

—∘O∘—

Acquire a piece of rope, cord, string, or lacing at least 2 feet (61 cm) in length. Sit in a quiet place where you feel comfortable. Near one end of the rope, tie a loose knot. Focus your attention completely on the process of tying the knot. When you've finished, tie another loose knot a few inches from the first knot. Then tie another. * Work slowly and methodically, keeping your attention on your task. If your mind starts to wander or you catch yourself becoming bored, take a deep breath and exhale. Then bring your attention back to the details of your task. * Appreciate the dexterity with which your fingers function. Notice the numerous movements you must make to create each knot. Continue the process until you've tied as many knots as you can in the piece of rope. * Now, reverse the process and begin untying the knots one at a time. Work slowly and methodically, keeping your attention on what you're doing. * When you've untied all the knots, repeat the process.

....

....

....

....

....

....

....

....

....

....

....

....

....

....

....

....

....

....

....

∽ Because meditation shifts your focus to the here and now, it can help you stick with a task and see it through to completion. This has positive implications for job satisfaction and performance —whether you're doing repetitious, routine tasks or making executive decisions— and for producing outcomes as well.

Don't Meditate if You Feel Desperate

Desperation blocks meditation. Close your eyes. Take a few slow, deep breaths. As you inhale, feel yourself beginning to relax; as you exhale, let the desperation go. Ask your Higher Self to lift it from you. When you feel free, meditate.

Buddhist tradition teaches an ancient concept known as "loving-kindness," which involves compassion and appreciation for all living creatures. As the Dalai Lama explains, "My religion is kindness."

MEDITATIONS TO IMPROVE RELATIONSHIPS

Silence Judgment to Reduce Relationship Stress

The following practice helps you become aware of the judgments you make every day. By paying attention to how you judge others, you can reduce the stress you experience when relating to other people and ease tensions with family members, partners, and coworkers.

—o○o—

Notice each time you make a verbal or mental judgment about someone else. That idiot pulled right out in front of me! That woman is so fat, how can she let herself get that way? He's stupid to believe that crazy idea. And so on... ✶ Notice each time you use these words: should, must, ought to, got to, have to, need to. Just observe what you say and think. Each time you catch yourself judging or criticizing someone, simply acknowledge it by mentally saying judgment. ✶ Don't judge or blame yourself for having judgmental thoughts. In time, you'll discover that you aren't as quick to find fault with others. Your desire to change them lessens. You can observe the people in your life without criticizing them or judging them to be wrong. ✶ You'll also find that your own stress level diminishes, as does the tension between you and other people. Make this practice a part of your everyday life.

Stress can adversely impact our relationships with the people in our lives, so it's no surprise that meditation, by reducing stress and anxiety, can help us get along better with loved ones, coworkers, and friends.

We have all had encounters with the Higher Self... although we may have difficulty expressing this after the fact. You might experience it during times of crisis, when you sense something wiser and more powerful than your ordinary human self protecting and guiding you. Or, you may experience it during times of ecstasy, when you sense a loving and expansive "presence" joyfully celebrating with you. During such times you realize you are not alone, that "someone" is with you.

In her book *The Art of Sexual Ecstasy*, Margo Anand writes, "Meditation helps you bring heightened awareness to the body, heart, and mind and to tune these three aspects of your being into a harmony that allows higher, more intense levels of pleasurable experience."

Build Sexual Energy

When the sacral chakra is blocked or otherwise imbalanced, various types of sexual dysfunction can result. The following meditation stimulates the flow of energy into the sacral chakra to increase sexual vitality.

—○O○—

Sit or lie comfortably with your eyes closed. Take a deep breath and exhale. Do this two more times. Bring your attention to the root chakra, the energy center located at the base of your spine. Imagine a spark of fire glowing at this part of your body. Deepen your breathing, and as you do, sense this spark burning more brightly. ✶ Feel the pleasing warmth generated by the fire. Sense its red-orange glow spreading through the lower part of your body. See or sense the fire swelling upward, into your sacral chakra. ✶ Feel this part of your body becoming energized and enlivened by the fire. Allow sensual feelings to emerge and gradually intensify. Rather than being localized in the genitals, these pleasurable feelings radiate through your hips and abdomen. ✶ When you're ready, sense the fire slowly diminishing, burning down until only a bed of hot coals remains at the base of your spine. Open your eyes.

MEDITATION BELONGS TO ALL OF US

Everyone can meditate and everyone can attain unlimited benefits from its practice. You can meditate regardless of your physical, mental, or emotional condition. Your age, race, gender, and nationality don't matter. You do not need to be an ascetic, a monk, or a sadhu (ascetic) to meditate.

Become a Better Receiver

By letting someone give to you, you honor the giver and share his/her joy. Everyone gains, and no one loses.

———o0o———

Sit or lie comfortably, with your eyes closed. Take a deep breath and exhale. Do this two more times. After you are relaxed, mentally count down from seven to one, relaxing more deeply with each count.
⋆ On the count of one, find yourself in your Safe Place. Feel the beauty, love, blessed solitude, or enchantment of this place. Invite your Higher Self to join you. Now, both of you stand (in the meditation). Turn your back to your Higher Self. Your Higher Self will place its hands on your back.
⋆ Very slowly drop backward while your Higher Self supports you. Lean all your weight against your Higher Self. Lean back further and further until you are completely reliant on your Higher Self's support.
⋆ After a while, your Higher Self will gently bring you back to an upright position. Thank your Higher Self and embrace. Ask for help to further heal your resistances to receiving from others. ⋆ Now, close your mental eyes and mentally count from one to five. On the count of five, open your physical eyes and return.

Disputes with the people we know often arise from the judgments we've made about them. When we point fingers and judge other people to be wrong, we experience frustration, disappointment, anger, anxiety, or other unpleasant emotions.

Virtually Anyone Can Meditate

The belief that meditation's benefits come only after years of effort is erroneous. Every time you sit in meditation you achieve results: some may be what you expect; others, not.

"When you change the way you look at things,
the things you look at change."

~ *Best-selling author Dr. Wayne Dyer*

MEDITATIONS TO
ATTRACT WHAT
YOU WANT IN LIFE

Attract Whatever You Desire
While You Sleep

Although you're not aware of what's actually taking place, you can choose what you want your unconscious to work on while you sleep. You can program your mind to attract health, prosperity, a relationship—whatever you desire.

—o0o—

Just before falling asleep, decide what you want to work on while you sleep. Do you seek healing? Is there something you want to learn more about or an issue you wish to resolve? Would you like to manifest something in your life? Be specific. ✿ Hold the desire in your mind as you drift off to sleep. Visualize the desire. Feel it. ✿ When you wake in the morning, immediately write down what you remember of any dreams you may have had. If you like, draw pictures of what you can recall.

Meditation enables you to eliminate confusion, focus your mind, and clarify your intentions.

Although some people may choose to meditate for extended periods of time, and some meditations take longer than others, you'll notice benefits even if you spend only ten minutes a day meditating.

When you order something from a catalog or online, you must clearly stipulate what you want—item number, size, color, quantity, and so on. The same holds true when you "order" something from the universe. If you aren't clear about what you intend to attract, you may end up with something you didn't expect or want.

Tap the Attracting Power of Sex

According to Tantric Yoga, a spiritual practice used in the East
for 6,000 years, sexual orgasm is one of the most powerful forces
we can experience. This waking meditation will be far more effective
if you practice it with someone you love.

———o0o———

Before undertaking this meditation, discuss with your partner what
one, or both, of you wish to attract—a new job, a home, good health,
whatever you desire. Choose only one thing at a time. * Engage in sex.
Take your time and make the act an expression of your mutual love.
Feel love's tenderness, the divine dance of ebb and flow, the blending
of two energy forces becoming one. As you approach climax,
hold in your minds a mental image of what you intend to attract.
* As you reach orgasm, feel the joy of having received your wish,
and then release it. The force of your physical release propels your
intention out into the universe like a rocket. Let the image totally go.
Do not think about or discuss your intention. Relax; enjoy each
other and the blissful state of calm that follows.

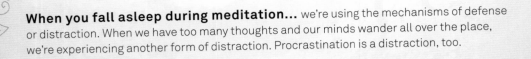

When you fall asleep during meditation... we're using the mechanisms of defense or distraction. When we have too many thoughts and our minds wander all over the place, we're experiencing another form of distraction. Procrastination is a distraction, too.

The Most Powerful Meditation Ever (And the Most Difficult)

When done from a place of integrity (meaning being the adult you are, not the child or adolescent you may sometimes play), this meditation can attract anything you desire into your life or release anything from it that you don't want.

———○O○———

Sit or lie comfortably, with your eyes closed. Take a deep breath and exhale. Do this two more times. After you are relaxed, mentally count down from seven to one, relaxing more deeply with each count.

✻ On the count of one, find yourself in your Safe Place. Invite your Higher Self to join you. With integrity and sincerity—and without desperation, self-pity, or doubt—ask your Higher Self for help.

✻ Be willing to receive the help you've requested. Don't try to direct, judge, or predict how the help will come or how your request will materialize. Just allow it to do so. When you feel ready, close your mental eyes and mentally count from one to five. On the count of five, open your physical eyes and return.

Today's researchers at major universities and medical facilities worldwide continue to discover new ways to utilize meditation's therapeutic powers, from promoting stem cell growth to increasing brain size. We may have just begun to tap meditation's abilities to heal body, mind, and spirit.

MANIFEST WITH ENDORPHINS

In their book *The 7 Secrets of Synchronicity*, Trish and Rob MacGregor explain it this way: "When we are focused, passionate, pushing our limits, our brains release endorphins. Research indicates this happens during sex, childbirth, strenuous exercise, meditation, and intense creative work. If you visualize what you want when endorphins are rushing through you, desires manifest more quickly. It's as if the endorphins somehow help connect you to the powerful source of who you really are, and the potential of who you can become."

"Meditation also quiets your *inner judge*."

⌒ *the voice of discouragement that can block creative attempts*

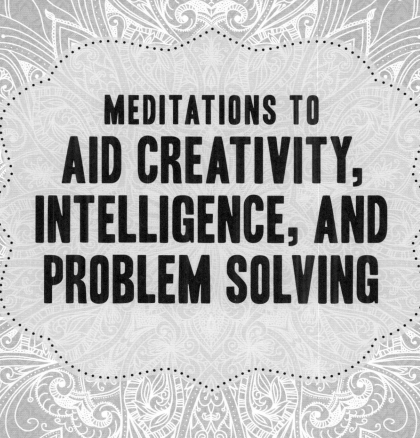

MEDITATIONS TO AID CREATIVITY, INTELLIGENCE, AND PROBLEM SOLVING

Night Whispers:
Gain Creative Inspiration at Night

The magic in the night air seems to bathe away any blocks and resistances
you may be experiencing, and the stars and moon serve as steady allies
in this waking meditation. Devote a few evenings, weather allowing,
to sitting outside in silence without distractions.

—o0o—

Sit quietly. Close your eyes for a little while and allow the stillness to quiet
your mental noise. Feel your heartbeat settling into a calm, easy pace.
Your breathing becomes slower, deeper, more refined. ✷ You may feel some
restlessness temporarily. That's okay. If you're not used to being alone outside
at night the experience may seem strange or even a little scary at first.
Open your eyes when you feel ready. Just sit, quietly. Feel the peace, the
softness, the grandeur that is Night. Gaze at the moon and stars. ✷ Don't try
to control what presents itself to you; just let whatever comes, come. On your
notepad, jot down what comes to you, so you won't forget later. Don't censor
what presents itself to you; just note it and keep your mind open. ✷ Spend
as long as you like experiencing the magical, mystical energy of the
Night and your own awakening inspiration. When you're ready to "call
it an evening," thank the Night, and go indoors.

~ The U.S. military is exploring meditation as a way to treat post-traumatic stress disorder and traumatic brain injury. The Defense Department spent $5 million in 2008 researching meditation and other complementary healing modalities.

LEARN
FROM OUR
ANCESTORS

Modern Westerners have lost an ability our ancestors long ago possessed: the ability to "read" everyday things around us and to glean answers from them. Our ancestors knew that nature provided not only for our basic needs but also the answers to life's mysteries and our mundane questions as well. Animal behavior, weather patterns, and other symbols in nature offered insights and inspiration.

Daily meditation, as Sara Lazar, PhD, and fellow researchers at Massachusetts General Hospital discovered in 2005, actually thickens the parts of the brain's cerebral cortex that are responsible for decision making.

The Answer Box: Resolve Problems, Get Answers

This meditation draws on the rituals of ancient peoples—including the Egyptians, Maya, Chinese, and Tibetans—who buried boxes filled with prayers and other requests in the earth in order to gain answers and assistance.

——o0o——

Find an old, antique-looking box with a lid. Use this box only for the purposes described in this meditation. On a piece of paper write a question, a problem, or an issue for which you'd like an answer or guidance. Place it in your Answer Box. ✶ Sit or lie comfortably, with your eyes closed. Take a deep breath and exhale. Do this two more times. When you feel relaxed, mentally count down from seven to one, relaxing more deeply with each count. On the count of one, find yourself in a beautiful garden. Trees and flowers of all kinds delight your senses. Let this be a place of enchantment for you. In your hands you hold a box. This box contains the piece of paper on which you've written your question, problem, or request. Find a place where you can bury the box. With your hands, start digging a hole in the earth. ✶ Place the box carefully in the ground, and then cover it with dirt. By burying the box, you are allowing your concern to gestate—like a seed planted in the soil—until it's ready to burst forth in blossom at a later date. When you've finished, close your mental eyes and sit quietly. Then, mentally count from one to five. On the count of five, open your physical eyes and return. ✶ Take the box with your written request in it and secret it someplace in your home—a closet, the basement or attic, or another place where it will be hidden from view.

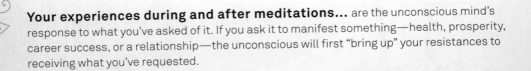

Your experiences during and after meditations... are the unconscious mind's response to what you've asked of it. If you ask it to manifest something—health, prosperity, career success, or a relationship—the unconscious will first "bring up" your resistances to receiving what you've requested.

....

....

....

....

....

....

....

....

....

Watch Clouds to
Expand Creativity and Imagination

Do the following meditation to help you think outside the box and
arrive at creative solutions to problems.

—o0o—

Lie on your back outdoors, in a place where you feel comfortable.
Relax and empty your mind of thoughts as you gaze up at the sky.
Choose a cloud and observe it calmly. Do you perceive images or
shapes in it? Does it look like an animal, a car, a tree, or something
else? ✱ As the cloud drifts across the sky, watch it slowly change
shape. What does it remind you of now? Keep observing the cloud as
it shifts its shape again and again. Give your imagination free rein.
✱ Choose another cloud and watch it transform itself into various
images. What do they look like to you? If other thoughts arise into
your awareness, simply let them go and focus your attention again
on the clouds. Continue doing this for as long as you like.

How can you communicate with your unconscious? The unconscious doesn't speak to us in English, French, Spanish, or any other human tongue—it uses the language of myth, metaphor, archetype, and symbol, according to Swiss analyst Carl Jung.

ZEN BUDDHISM

Often contemplation is associated with Zen Buddhism, but it has been a part of many spiritual practices worldwide for millennia. Contemplation involves focusing on an idea, a question, a word, or a phrase in order to gain a deeper understanding of it. According to Father Thomas Keating, founder of Contemplative Outreach, Ltd., contemplation gives us "a sense of interconnectedness with all creation." Spiritual teacher, author, artist, and composer Sri Chinmoy says, "When we are contemplating we feel that we are holding within ourselves the entire universe with all its infinite light, peace, bliss, and truth."

Each of us has the power to change anything and everything—no exceptions.

MEDITATIONS TO HEAL THE PLANET

Hang Prayer Flags to
Send Blessings Around the World

Traditional Tibetan prayer flags are made in five colors—red, yellow, green, blue, and white—that correspond to the five elements that Tibetans believe compose our world. However, you may choose cloth of whatever color(s) you prefer.

——∘O∘——

Cut one or more squares of colored cloth—as many as you like—each about 8 inches (20 cm) square. Using a felt marker with permanent ink, write a prayer or blessing on one piece of cloth. As you write, contemplate your intentions. ✱ Keep your thoughts focused on what you are writing or drawing—don't let your mind wander. When you've finished, write another prayer or blessing on a second piece of cloth. Continue writing prayers—one per flag—until you're satisfied that you've stated all your intentions. After you've created several prayer flags, sew, pin, or otherwise attach the squares of colored cloth to a piece of string, so they look like laundry hanging on a clothesline. ✱ Fasten them to your home, a tree, a fence, or another place where they can blow in the breeze. As the wind catches the flags and causes them to flutter, imagine your blessings drifting on the wind to the four corners of Earth. ✱ Imagine your prayers healing the world. When the flags have faded so they can no longer be read, take them down and create more.

~~ **Deva** is a Sanskrit word that means "shining one." In the natural world, devas are nonphysical beings who are responsible for the growth, maintenance, nurturance, and evolution of plants and animals.

MYTHS OF MEDITATION

The belief that meditative practices are the sole domain of an esoteric few who commit themselves to untold years sitting in isolated caves or sequestered in rarefied ashrams is false. Although some people seek "enlightenment" in this manner, that is a choice, not a requirement.

Five thousand years ago, the authors of the Hindu sacred texts known as the Vedas recorded the first written discussions of meditation practices.

Observe Water to Perceive Life Energy

Wilhelm Reich, an Austrian-born psychologist and colleague of Freud's in the 1920s, spent his later years in the United States studying and writing about a universal life energy he referred to as orgone. This energy, which Chinese medicine calls qi or chi, flows through the earth and all living things.

———∘O∘———

Sit near a lake, pond, stream, or other body of water. Relax, and gently ease all thoughts out of your mind as you gaze at the water. Instead of staring into the water, cast your gaze slightly above the water's surface. ✦ Notice a slight shimmering or bluish haze rippling just above the surface of the water. Keep watching, letting your vision relax and even blur a bit. You'll notice the bluish haze moves in a circular pattern. ✦ What you are observing is orgone, or qi. This energy is also moving through you, connecting you with everything else on Earth. As you continue gazing at the water, feel this life energy flowing in your body with each breath you take. Feel yourself becoming more calm and relaxed. ✦ Sit for as long as you like, observing this energy and feeling your connection with all life on Earth.

When you bring more love into your life... the world becomes more loving. When you heal yourself, the world becomes more healed. You can choose to actively engage the world or sit in meditation: it doesn't matter. The world will be a better place because of who you are, not what you do.

ABOUT THE AUTHORS

DR. MARTIN HART is the founder and president of the American Society of Alternative Therapists (ASAT™) and has been in private counseling and alternative health education for more than thirty-five years. Since 1978, Dr. Hart has conducted workshops and lectures throughout the United States and the world on meditation and other life-enhancing subjects. He has taught at some of the largest corporations in Asia, as well as top colleges and research facilities. In the late 1980s, he incorporated a series of unique healing modalities based on his successful counseling practice into a healing concept called ASAT C.O.R.E. Counseling, which, among other things, incorporates specifically designed meditations into a highly effective counseling approach. "Through ASAT™ C.O.R.E. Counseling, my students and I have seen the lives of thousands of our clients blossom and grow in remarkable ways. They are crafting exceptional lives that are fun, empowering, and even magical. Where struggle and conflict once flourished in their lives, now challenge and elegance thrive. And all this has happened in a remarkably short period of time. Our clients report being happier, healthier, more successful, and more productive, and their lives are taking on a kind of magic marked by glorious synchronicities." As a result of the efficacy of this approach, Dr. Hart started training ASAT C.O.R.E. counselors in 1990 through live trainings and home study. There are now more than 1,700 certified ASAT C.O.R.E. counselors throughout the world. Dr. Hart still travels the United States and the world, conducting his trainings as well as other related lectures and workshops. His courses and workshops have been featured in the *Wall Street Journal, Boston Globe, London Sunday Telegraph*, and other publications. He has also appeared on national and international television and radio programs discussing his unique work. To contact him regarding his trainings and workshops, send an email to asat@asat.org or visit ASAT's website at www.asat.org.

SKYE ALEXANDER is the author of more than thirty books and healing card decks, including *The Pocket Encyclopedia of Healing Touch Therapies*, *10-Minute Feng Shui,* and *The Care and Feeding of Your Chi*. Meditation and yoga have been part of her daily regimen for thirty-five years. You can visit her website and blog at www.skyealexander.com.